I Like My Family

By Margo Austen

Scott Foresman
is an imprint of

Glenview, Illinois • Boston, Massachusetts • Mesa, Arizona
Shoreview, Minnesota • Upper Saddle River, New Jersey

ISBN 13: 978-0-328-39733-4
ISBN 10:   0-328-39733-4

11 12 13 14 15 V010 17 16 15 14 13

I like my mom.

I like my dad.

I like my sister.

I like my brother.

I like my dog.

I like my family.